Bilingual Edition

Edición bilingüe

# Let's Draw a
# Fire Truck with Shapes

## Vamos a dibujar un
## camión de bomberos
## usando figuras

Joanne Randolph
Illustrations by Emily Muschinske

Traducción al español:
Mauricio Velázquez de León

The Rosen Publishing Group's
PowerStart Press™ & **Editorial Buenas Letras**™
New York

*In memory of The Bruiser—a dog who sometimes thought he was a fire truck*

Published in 2005 by The Rosen Publishing Group, Inc.
29 East 21st Street, New York, NY 10010

First Edition

Book Design: Emily Muschinske

Photo Credits: p. 23 © Peter Turnley/CORBIS.

Library of Congress Cataloging-in-Publication Data
Randolph, Joanne.
Let's draw a fire truck with shapes = Vamos a dibujar un camión de bomberos usando figuras / Joanne Randolph ; illustrations by Emily Muschinske ; translated by Mauricio Velázquez de León.
    p. cm. — (Let's draw with shapes = Vamos a dibujar con figuras)
Includes index.
ISBN 1-4042-7556-8 (library binding)
1. Fire engines in art—Juvenile literature. 2. Drawing—Technique—Juvenile literature. I. Title: Vamos a dibujar un camión de bomberos usando figuras. II. Muschinske, Emily, ill. III. Title. IV. Let's draw with shapes.

NC825.T76R358 2005b
743'.89629224—dc22
                                                    2004009838


Manufactured in the United States of America


Due to the changing nature of Internet links, PowerStart Press has developed an online list of Web sites related to the subject of this book. This site is updated regularly. Please use this link to access the list:
http://www.buenasletraslinks.com/ldwsh/bomberos

# Contents

1 Let's Draw a Fire Truck     4

2 Color in Your Fire Truck     20

3 Fighting Fires     22

Words to Know     24

Colors/Shapes     24

Index     24

# Contenido

1 Vamos a dibujar un camión de bomberos     4

2 Colorea tu camión de bomberos     20

3 Apagando incendios     22

Palabras que debes saber     24

Colores/Figuras     24

Índice     24

Draw a red rectangle for the back of your fire truck. Add four red rectangles and a square to your fire truck.

---

Dibuja la parte trasera de tu camión de bomberos trazando un rectángulo rojo. Agrega cuatro rectángulos y un cuadrado.

4

Add an orange square to make the front of your fire truck. Draw an orange rectangle for the bumper.

---

Agrega un cuadrado anaranjado para hacer el frente de tu camión. Dibuja el parachoques trazando un rectángulo.

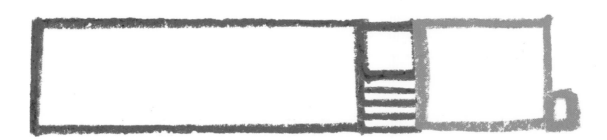

Draw a yellow rectangle for the hose of your fire truck. Add nine rectangles for the ladder of your fire truck.

Dibuja un rectángulo amarillo para la manguera de tu camión de bomberos. Agrega nueve rectángulos para hacer la escalera.

9

Add two green rectangles for the windows on your fire truck. Draw a circle for a light on your fire truck.

---

Agrega dos rectángulos verdes para dibujar las ventanas. Dibuja un círculo para hacer el faro de tu camión de bomberos.

Draw a blue square and a blue rectangle on the back of your fire truck. Add two small blue circles, too.

---

Dibuja un rectángulo y un cuadrado de color azul en la parte trasera del camión. Agrega dos círculos azules pequeños.

13

Add two purple rectangles and a purple circle to the back part of your fire truck.

Dibuja dos rectángulos y un círculo de color violeta en la parte trasera de tu camión de bomberos.

Draw a pink triangle on the back of your fire truck.

---

Dibuja un triángulo rosa a la parte trasera de tu camión de bomberos.

Add two large black circles and two small black circles for the wheels on your fire truck.

---

Agrega las ruedas a tu camión de bomberos. Dibuja dos círculos negros grandes y dos círculos pequeños.

Color in your fire truck.

---

Colorea tu camión
de bomberos.

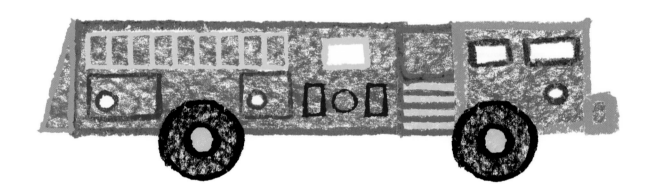

21

Fire trucks are used to fight fires every day.

---

Todos los días, los camiones de bomberos se usan para apagar incendios.

# Words to Know/Palabras que debes saber

bumper/
parachoques

hose/manguera

ladder/escalera

wheel/rueda

## Colors/ Colores

 red/rojo

orange/anaranjado

yellow/amarillo

 green/verde

 blue/azul

 purple/violeta

pink/rosa

 black/negro

## Shapes/ Figuras

○ circle/círculo

□ square/cuadrado

△ triangle/triángulo

▭ rectangle/rectángulo

⬭ oval/óvalo

⌒ half circle/semicírculo

# Index

**B**
bumper, 6

**F**
fires, 22

**H**
hose, 8

**L**
ladder, 8
light, 10

**W**
wheels, 18
windows, 10

# Índice

**E**
escalera, 8

**I**
incendios, 22

**M**
manguera, 8

**R**
ruedas, 18

**P**
parachoques, 6

**V**
ventanas, 10